The Elements of Mindfulness

Also by Scott Rogers

Mindful Parenting:
Meditations, Verses and Visualizations for a More Joyful Life

Mindfulness for Law Students:
Using the Power of Mindful Awareness to Achieve Balance and Success in Law School

The Six-Minute Solution:
A Mindfulness Primer for Attorneys

Mindfulness and Professional Responsibility:
A Handbook for Integrating Mindfulness into the Law School Classroom

Attending: A Physician's Introduction to Mindfulness

Mindfulness, Balance & The Lawyer's Brain
(Florida CLE Course Book and Audio Recording)

Child Is the Cosmos:
Mindful Parenting Visualizations
(Audio Recording)

The Elements of Mindfulness

An Invitation to Explore the Nature of
Waking Up to the Present Moment
. . . and Staying Awake

Scott L. Rogers

Mindful Living Press
2017

© 2017. Scott L. Rogers. All rights reserved.

No part of this book may be used or reproduced in any manner whatsoever without the written permission of the publisher. Published in the United States of America. For information, contact Mindful Living Press, 800 West Avenue, Suite C-1, Miami Beach, FL 33139.

SoBe Mindful® is a registered trademark of the Institute for Mindfulness Studies.

Cover design: Cathy Gibbs Thornton

Copy editor: Melissa Hayes

Library of Congress Control Number: 2017913593

ISBN: 978-0-9773455-7-1

First Printing, August 2017

10 9 8 7 6 5 4 3 2

FOR

Paul and Marte

*In gratitude for your support,
and for a cherished friendship
that enriches my life,
day by day,
moment by moment.*

IN LOVING MEMORY OF

Jason Michael Ryan Thornton

*Thank you for your love,
light, laughter, and your wisdom,
and for blessing our lives
beyond measure.
Your passion for life inspires us to
live each day to the fullest.*

Table of Contents

Acknowledgments ix
Introduction 1
Part I: Method
    1. The Elements of Mindfulness 17
    2. Exploring the Elements: Doing 41
    3. Exploring the Elements: Being 63
    4. The Secondary Elements 111
Part II: Practice
    5. The SoBe Mindful Flow and Punctuated Practice 149
        SoBe Mindful Stop 157
        SoBe Mindful Minute 161
        SoBe Mindful Now 165
    6. Planned Practices 169
        SoBe Mindful Sunrise 173
        SoBe Mindful & Kind 185
        SoBe Mindful & Grateful 201

Answers to Common Questions 206
Recommended Reading 210
About the Author 211
About the Illustrator 213
SoBe Mindful Tools and Toys 214

Acknowledgments

During the course of the ten years during which this book germinated, I have had the joy of meeting many wonderful people from whom I have learned, and with whom I have had the pleasure of collaborating.

I am grateful to Tammy Sifre for our early discussions of the subject matter of this book and for many years of the truest form of friendship. Thank you Keryn Breiterman-Loader and Christina Sava for your help reducing the many ideas and images found in this book into a more manageable form.

Thank you, Amishi Jha, for your trust, integrity, and friendship. Our work developing, delivering, and assessing the efficacy of mindfulness training to a diversity of groups has allowed me to explore a larger container for the skillful articulation and sharing of mindfulness practices.

I am immensely grateful to Patricia White, dean of the University of Miami School of Law, where I have the privilege of teaching mindfulness to law students. Your invitation to join the law school faculty opened a door that allows me to share mindfulness each year with hundreds of students at the law school and across the university. The ongoing grappling with, and evolution of, mindfulness course curricula and opportunity to explore mindfulness with students and faculty has expanded my skills and offers me invaluable insights and perspectives.

I am indebted to the generous colleagues and students who help support the Mindfulness in Law Program by collaborating with me in teaching mindfulness classes—Jan Jacobowitz, Raquel Matas, and Rob Rosen—infusing mindfulness into clinics—Bernie Perlmutter, Kele Stewart, Robert Latham, Rebecca Sharpless, Romy Lerner, JoNel Newman, Melissa Swain, Caroline Bettinger-Lopez, and Patricia Redmond—and by facilitating Mindful Spaces on the law school campus—Vanessa Alpizar, Joy Clayton, Dale Dobuler, Jonathan Erbstein, Jason Goldstein, Geena Kandel, Deb Martin, Rob Rosen, Alex Schimel, Janet Stearns, Luevenia Sterling, and Rachel Tuckerman, and across the university—David Lee, Janet Konefal, Kelly Miller, Vera Spika, Jodi Sypher, and Hope Torrents. The creative ways we have collaborated on the development of course curricula and of Mindful Spaces has inspired deep and ongoing reflection on offering mindfulness practice in accessible and meaningful forms.

So too, I am grateful to friends and colleagues who have visited with students in the Mindfulness in Law class over the past five years to elevate their understanding of mindfulness and the ways it can be integrated into their professional lives. Thank you Alan Gold, Lance Harke, Dan Harris, Alice Lash, Chris McAliley, Tony Recio, Tim Ryan, Sharon Salzberg, Christina Sava, Paul Singerman, Harley Tropin, and Steven Zuckerman. And to Harley and Sherry Tropin, Paul and Marte Singerman, Adam and Jessica Moskowitz, Ed Rubinoff, and the law firms Berger Singerman and Kozyak, Tropin and Throckmorton, thank you for your generous support.

I have in earlier books thanked the many friends and colleagues who have and continue to inspire me. Among them, I wish to express my deep gratitude and appreciation to Alan Gold—a mentor, benefactor, and friend whose wise counsel has meant more to me than I could ever convey. You and Susan are very special to me, and your friendship and kindness touch me deeply. Had I completed this book earlier, I would have liked very much to discuss and share it with Melvin Rubin, a dear friend and champion. In Mel's passing I, along with so many others, carry a sense of deep loss and sadness. If the Elements upon which this book is premised mean anything, it is in their reminder of the joy of connection, the impermanence of life, and the mystery of renewal. Mel—you and Susan traveled the world, and I can only imagine the countless sunrises and sunsets, tropical and balmy breezes, forests and gardens, and cloud-filled skies you came across in your many adventures.

Thank you, Paul and Andrea Silitsky, for your friendship and encouragement in the final stages of development of the SoBe Mindful Method and for your interest in sharing it with others, along with your important work increasing the reach of meditation practice within our community.

I have had the good fortune to learn from wonderful teachers, whose insight and guidance has deepened my personal practice and, in turn, informed the richness of my own teaching, which is nothing more than their teachings, and that of their teachings, in a less realized form. I will always be grateful to Fred Eppsteiner, Rosemary Barkett, Sharon Salzberg, Fletcher Baldwin, Ram Dass, Arvey Rogers, and Thich Nhat Hanh. Each of them has imparted to me the heart of wise, compassionate, and engaged teaching. Ben Rogers, my grandfather, a true bodhisattva, taught me by living a life of nothing but love. And the love of his life, my grandmother, Julie Rogers, has in ways too numerous to mention and too elusive to convey, established that there is more to this world than one can know, and the heart of it all is gratitude.

As often as possible I head to Carmel, California, with my very dear and precious Aunt (Ant) Regina for a little relaxation and restoration. There is no one in the world I have ever or could ever know who more fully lives a life of service, and whose seemingly effortless expressions of empathy, compassion, action, and wisdom have taught me what it is to live a meaningful life and make the world a better place. I hope that each day I move a little closer to the space you inhabit. Thank you for your support and love, as I would not be doing the work I love were it not for you, and it is this work that has established the foundation for the development of this book.

Thank you, Paul Singerman, Marte Singerman, Robin Delgado, Chris McAliley, Arvey Rogers, Joan Rogers, Alice Lash, Stacey Edelman, Pam Rogers, Millie Rogers, and Rose Rogers for taking the time to review this manuscript, and for your helpful comments. Thank you, Melissa Hayes, for your expert eye. And thank you, Cathy Thornton, for so many years of fruitful collaboration, and for doing such a splendid job developing imagery to breathe life into the ideas and practices conveyed throughout this book.

Each morning's meditation begins with a turning of my mind and heart to my parents, Susan and Arvey, to my sisters, Stacey and Shana, to my daughters, Millie and Rose, and to my wife, Pam. Where would I be—could I be—without you? We have already begun to pass from this Earth and the moments of our togetherness grow more precious with every passing day. There can be no greater feeling of connection, affection, and gratitude than that which I have for you.

Introduction

Remembering

This book is about remembering, and waking up when we forget. While many books on mindfulness offer the reader information about mindfulness and how to practice it, this book is a little different. In it, you will not find an in-depth discussion of mindfulness. There is no review of the science of mindfulness and no claims are made for its benefits.

This book appreciates the many superb treatments of mindfulness that are available and takes another path. What makes it different is that its contents are the mindfulness practice.

Most important, this book is intended to render itself irrelevant. The more fully you review and practice its contents, the more completely it consumes itself. Its utility is to equip you and then it is your responsibility to let go.

And here is a secret. There is nothing in this book that you do not already know. It's that we tend to forget important things, like we are already awake, that we have all that we need, that we are deeply connected to one another . . . that we can stop trying so hard.

This is a book that helps us remember.

The SoBe Mindful Invitation

Most people recognize the importance of taking time now and again to sidestep the busyness of life, to relax and recharge. There is an ache to slow down, to reset, and to replenish a store of energy, enthusiasm, focus, and passion that is so quickly depleted in today's highly distracted, fast-paced, and changing world.

And yet, few people have an easy time letting go for a few minutes of the busyness of life and just being present. It's not for want of knowing how. Whether it's taking a leisurely walk, sitting with a cup of tea, or meditating for ten minutes, there is something about "slowing down" that is hard to do. I suspect this is because these are not things to "do" as much as they are ways to "be," yet we keep trying to "do" them.

One form of "being present" that transcends the ages is sitting and paying attention to an object such as the breath. Seemingly not much going on, boring even. But the extraordinary gift this practice offers is quickly realized by those who persevere. And, more recently, an understanding of why this practice may be beneficial to our cognitive, emotional, and physical well-being is being reported in medical and scientific journals.

Still, even when one has a taste of these benefits from their direct experience, or feels a strong urge to "slow down," or has been warned that if they do not find a way to "slow down" or "take it easy," their physical health may be in jeopardy, it can remain a great challenge. I know many meditators who marvel over how easy it is to sit for hours when they go on retreat, how easy it is to sit for an hour after they return home from retreat, and then how, slowly but surely, their daily practice reverts to ten or fifteen minutes a day, and even that is sporadic.

I do not believe there is a prescribed amount of time one should sit—if one sits at all. We are all different, and everything in its time. But the common complaint, frequently couched as a regret, is the wish to sit longer, or to "just sit."

This book offers you a somewhat novel path to understanding and practicing mindfulness. In it you will learn to practice by connecting the elements of nature to the elements of your true nature, through imagery found just about everywhere in the world. In the beginning, you will learn to follow the book's guided practices and, in so doing, you will be practicing mindfulness. At the same time, because mindfulness invites you to show up for life just as you are—without a book, without needing anything—you will readily transfer what you are learning to other moments of your life, so that mindfulness arises spontaneously. Soon enough, you are able to put aside the book and integrate what you have been practicing into your day—your life.

This approach is known as the SoBe Mindful Method. But because the "method" is really a reminder of that which we already know, calling it a method makes it into more than it is. Just as we can make mindfulness into more than it is.

Meditation teachers have long offered pithy invitations to "just sit," "be present," and "wake up." If only we could follow such straightforward instructions. In much the same way, this book offers a similar invitation—"You want to be mindful . . . So Be Mindful." For this reason, I'll sometimes refer to it as the "SoBe Mindful invitation." After all, life is an invitation.

Much of what you will learn in this introduction to the SoBe Mindful Method consists of short mindfulness practice moments. These range from a few seconds to several minutes, and form the building blocks for both self-guided practices you can draw upon anytime, anywhere, and book-guided practices, many of which you will find in the SoBe Mindful book series that offers guided mindfulness practices tailored to specific contexts.

Mindfulness

Mindfulness is about paying attention to what is taking place in the present moment. It's about "waking up" and not missing the most important, satisfying, and consequential moments of your life. That is, not missing the moments of your life. The impediment to this is the steady stream of thoughts that run through our minds, interpreting our experience, and weaving stories about what has happened, what is happening, and what might happen next.

Our attention is drawn toward these thoughts, identifies with them, and often accepts them as true. As this happens, we forget where we truly are, what truly matters, and even why we are here.

Our thoughts begin calling the shots. If these thoughts were the product of deep wisdom and compassion, all would be well. But often they are merely a conditioned aspect of our nature. Trace back our life experiences (i.e., walk a mile in one's moccasins), and it makes sense that we persist in experiencing various agitating and worrisome thoughts. But that is very different from our thoughts making sense. The thinking mind, however, will never see beyond the trappings of its own conditioning. What is needed is that a part of us, outside of thought, can realize that thoughts are not facts but momentary expressions of mental activity. When this happens, we more readily discern which thoughts to attend to, and which to let pass, like clouds floating across the sky.

When we are able to shine the light of awareness onto the momentary activity of the mind, we gain clarity into the true nature of our experience. We see more clearly that the stories we are telling ourselves are mental elaborations borne out of forgetfulness—out of fear and anger, frustration, regret, and doubt. To draw upon the metaphor of clouds, it is as if the sun has arisen, revealing what had been a dark sky. Clouds that have been threatening are seen for what they are—momentary aspects of the natural world. It literally dawns on us that there is more going on than that which meets the mind.

A helpful means of learning to stay present, moment to moment, is the breath. Wisdom traditions for thousands of years have appreciated that, like the wind or a gentle breeze, the breath is always close by, arising, changing, and passing away. Thus, the breath is a reliable object upon which we can place our attention, and notice changes and fluctuations. Also, the breath plays a useful role in learning not to get carried away by every compelling and agitating thought that comes along and threatens to derail our attention. We resume our attending to the breath when we realize we stopped paying attention to it and fell into forgetfulness.

So mindfulness has something to do with staying awake and attending to what is actually arising in our lives. Sharon Salzberg offers us that mindfulness is telling the difference between what is taking place and the stories we tell ourselves about what is taking place. But if our thoughts have been conditioned by a lifetime of experience—if we have lived so much of our lives like a child trembling amid the lightning and thunder of a threatening sky—how are we to get out from under the bed, open our eyes, look courageously at the sky, and venture to step out into the world, so that we might learn what is really happening out there, what's really happening in here?

The answer resides in our body, our precious human body. While our thoughts come and go, our body is here—always here, now. And our body is very much connected to the earth, borne of the earth, and will one day return to the earth. And just as there is an endless stream of thoughts and feelings, so too is there an endless stream of sensations flowing through the body. Some are pleasant, some unpleasant.

And some are neither pleasant nor unpleasant, or are so subtle we barely notice them at all.

The sensations we feel, moment to moment, are the product of the health of our body and what it is experiencing in a very real and physical sense. We can tremble with chills, sweat with fever, swell with inflammation, and decline with disease and age. We are much like a tree that is also borne of this earth, sustained by this earth, and destined one day to return to the earth. The earth quakes and the tree trembles. The seasons pass and the tree's leaves change color, drop, and return. A fungus invades and the tree becomes ill. And given time, or the ax, the tree falls. Whereas the tree remains present for all that arises around, under, and within, we tend to do something about every tremor, every ache, every experience that doesn't feel good enough.

Through mindfulness practice, we learn that the pleasant, the unpleasant, and the neutral—and the stories we tell of the good, the bad, and the boring—are often momentary experiences that are the stuff of life. Rather than do something by seeking more of the good, pushing away the bad, and exciting the boring, we learn to notice the pleasant, observe the unpleasant, and become curious about the neutral. In time, we might even begin to appreciate that regarding our experiences as good, bad, or boring is nothing more than judgments that get in the way of genuinely and honestly experiencing the moments of our lives. As we do, we become better informed about when to take action because action is called for and when to allow things to be as they are. We learn what the tree knows only too well: Sensations come and go. Without even trying, the tree remains upright and stable, present, receptive, and vibrant.

Waking up the Natural Way

The above discussion of mindfulness draws upon various elements of nature: sun, wind, clouds, and trees, and of metaphors that help us learn more about ourselves. And because abstractions, ideas, images, and symbols are the currency of our thinking natures, it is no surprise that wisdom traditions have, for millennia, looked to nature and to the elements to help us better understand ourselves and make sense of the world.

The SoBe Mindful invitation draws upon these insights to help illuminate our understanding of mindfulness. Importantly—and as a fundamental premise upon which this book rests—these Elements are not to be looked upon solely as metaphors, but as our true nature. For where did we come from and where would we be were it not for the sun, wind, clouds, trees?

This book reminds us that when we see these elements, we are seeing ourselves. And, even more, when we see and experience them, we can find ourselves. They are our teachers and they point the way home. And if we are open to these pointers, we remember who we are, where we are, and we wake up to our true nature. We see more clearly and lovingly those with whom we are blessed to be journeying through life.

I live in Miami Beach, and the SoBe Mindful invitation derives from the scenery of South Beach. In fact, it was about twenty years ago that I had a profound experience while driving down US-1 that surely watered the seeds that have become this book. I'll share that experience with you briefly. I had been practicing mindfulness for about five years—sitting every morning, reading thoughtful books on the subject, and attending various workshops and retreats. The richness, beauty, and benefits of my practice were directly felt while sitting each morning and were seeping into the rest of my day—my life. And while I "knew" that every moment was a moment to wake up, to be present for the natural unfolding of life, still the experience of "waking up" was reserved for the cushion. And then that changed. Nothing dramatic, nothing special; to the contrary. As I drove down US-1, my mind doing whatever it was doing, I looked out the windshield, beyond the traffic, and I saw a tree. And in that moment I woke up. The tree, the sun, the clouds, the breeze. Words cannot explain the experience; suffice it to say that this awakened in me an interest in the role of the natural elements in helping us to wake up—to see more clearly what is taking place before us, within us. And so the elements we will draw upon are the tree, wind, clouds, and sun.

You may be wondering where is South Beach's most famous element—the ocean. Well, not everyone has an ocean nearby. But everyone, wherever they live, has ready access to trees, clouds, the sun, and the wind. The SoBe Mindful invitation is open to everyone, and the elements selected serve that end.

In addition to the four primary elements of sun, clouds, wind, and tree, you will be introduced to two supplemental elements which play a related but slightly different role in the SoBe Mindful invitation. Once you meet the elements and begin practicing with them, you'll appreciate that every element in nature is part of the invitation. Mountains, lakes, waves, elephants, rain, flowers, and so on. Should you live in a part of the world where some of these other elements are abundant, you may find that bringing them into the practice will meaningfully enrich your experience. At the same time, a word of caution: "Enrich" can sometimes be a euphemism for adding unnecessary complexity. It's like reading a book on mindfulness and then, rather than practicing for fifteen minutes, spending five hours reading another book on mindfulness.

There was nothing about the tree I saw that spring afternoon on US-1 that was special. It was that I "saw" the tree. And, as I will share with you, the tree helped me to see.

Waking Up Is Hard to Do

Whether it's taking a leisurely walk, sitting with a cup of tea, or meditating, there is something about slowing down as an avenue to "waking up" that is hard to do. An important distinction can be drawn between "doing" and "being." It is one often raised in mindfulness discussions, and I raise it now because it touches on a practical aspect of this book.

Being versus doing—being present for life as it unfolds versus taking action and doing something to fix a problem with life's unfolding—is, for many, a challenge. Some who "do" a lot—task-driven, on the go, movers and shakers, who begin to feel the weight of always being in motion—may decide it's time to "do" a little less and "be" a little more. Some who spend a lot of time removed from the action—passive, open, going with the flow—may decide it's time to "do" a little more. We are all looking for balance, and this inquiry—framed as "doing mode" and "being mode"—can be helpful.

The SoBe Mindful invitation acknowledges this duality (no pun intended) and honors both while appreciating that it is a false dichotomy. Is the wind doing or being? Is a tree doing or being? Answering these curious questions is less important than reflecting on this. The sun, wind, a tree, the clouds—whether they are being or doing—*are not trying*.

"Doing" something imparts a quality of effort. In contrast, "being" present connotes the opposite—allowing. If "waking up" is hard to do, perhaps it's because it is not something we "do." This confusion can be borne out of the belief that we need to change things to find relief from suffering. We may find relief, but when we "do" something without having been present and attentive to our experience, the consequences are often shortsighted, short-lived, or fall short. Doing and being belong together, and mindfulness helps to cultivate this more perfect union. "Being" gets boring because we are born to "do." And "doing" gets exhausting because we are born to "be." The SoBe Mindful invitation explores ways of doing *and* being with the elements as a guide. For example, you'll learn what it means to "take" a breath and what it means to "observe" a breath. You'll practice two ways of consciously experiencing the breath and become proficient in shifting between the two. Ultimately, because breathing is happening regardless of whether we are taking or observing the breath, we glimpse the way the mind tricks us into making things into more than they are.

As you attend to and reflect on the SoBe Mindful invitation, you will notice moments of waking up that arise more naturally, spontaneously, and effortlessly. You will gain a penetrating clarity about what is arising in your life, and you will experience it with a greater equanimity and felt sense of ease. Challenging moments will be more bearable than you imagined, because your imagination is not calling the shots, and you will develop greater resilience. Importantly, this doesn't happen because of something you are learning or figuring out. Rather, it happens because you are less distracted, telling yourself fewer stories, and, as a direct result, more present and awake for the life you are living.

Getting Started

In the chapters that follow, you will be introduced to the four primary and two secondary elements. For each you will learn exercises and insights connecting the elements to the cultivation of mindfulness. These insights will become increasingly meaningful as you explore the practices offered in this book, and as you go about your day—ever so much more attentive to the presence of each element, both inside and outside. You'll find that inclining the mind in this way brings about a shift in perspective, in the quality of your attention, and in your connection to the moment unfolding before you.

Chapters 1 through 4 set forth the SoBe Mindful Method. Through simple imagery and brief explanation, you will be offered insights and instruction to develop your understanding of mindfulness and learn fundamental aspects of practice. At the outset, you will be encouraged to go outdoors and reinforce what you are learning, using nature's palette and clay.

Chapter 5 moves from method to practice as you learn the SoBe Mindful Flow, and draw upon it to experience "punctuated" mindfulness practice, a term I coined that refers to spontaneous moments when you wake up out of mindlessness and automatic pilot. As you will learn, the SoBe Mindful Method facilitates "waking up" out of automatic pilot and the SoBe Mindful Flow offers ways of practicing to further enrich and deepen these moments. You will also learn a series of easy-to-remember exercises that can be practiced as part of a daily routine, along with an approach for integrating practice across the span of a week.

Chapter 6 offers insight into how the SoBe Mindful Method relates to traditional forms of mindfulness practice. You will learn the SoBe Mindful Sunrise, a practice that stands on its own and can naturally flow into a mindfulness of body, breath, mind, and bare attention practice, as well as the SoBe Mindful & Kind, a lovingkindness practice, and SoBe Mindful & Grateful, a gratitude practice.

The method used to introduce you to these planned practices is known as "book-guided" practice, in that you follow the imagery set forth on the page to guide your practice. This approach is intended to illustrate and more fully inform your understanding of the practice, and forms the basis of the SoBe Mindful book series. However, for purposes of this book, you will not need to return to the book to practice these exercises, once you have learned them.

And because this book is intended to equip you to practice in a more spontaneous and natural way wherever you are—without any trying involved—it is my hope that the last time you open this book, it will be much like opening the wardrobe in C. S. Lewis's classic. You open the cover and fall into the beauty of the natural world—trees, wind, clouds, and the sun. After all, as Zen master Thich Nhat Hanh reminds us, isn't that what a book is made of anyway?

It's time to meet the Elements.

Three Tips for Getting the Most Out of This Book

Take Your Time: This book can be read at a fast pace. Instead, take your time as you review it, reflecting on its methods, insights, and practices.

Stop: Many of the practices you will learn can be applied while you are in motion; for example, walking outdoors. It can be very helpful to literally "stop" or slow down while reflecting upon or engaging in an exercise, as this allows you to more fully experience the richness of the offering and to reinforce its practice.

Enjoy: Life is serious business and mindfulness is a serious practice. And both are meant to be enjoyed, to be a source of play, of growth, of inspiration.

Part I

Method

Chapter 1

The Elements of Mindfulness

Meet the Elements

The SoBe Mindful Method establishes the foundation for an accessible and memorable approach to practicing mindfulness. It is grounded in four Elements found in nature.

In this chapter, you will be introduced to these Elements and what they represent. Then you will learn mindfulness insights associated with each Element.

Read through this short chapter slowly, as its imagery and insights form the foundation for the SoBe Mindful Method.

Tree

Wind

Clouds

Sun

What the Elements Represent

Now that you know the four Elements, it's time to learn what they represent.

As you'll come to see, each represents a fundamental aspect of our true nature, and of the mindfulness practice.

Tree = The Body

Wind = Breath

Clouds = Thoughts and Feelings

Sun = Awareness

Mindfulness Insights and the Elements

There are several reasons why the Tree, Wind, Clouds, and Sun comprise the four Primary Elements.

One is that they are a part of everyday life. You will experience them practically every day.

Another is that they serve as metaphors for our capacity to be present, to wake up, and to remain steady in the here and now. In this regard, you will notice them within yourself practically every day.

We can learn from them, and they help us remember.

A Tree

A Tree represents the Body.

A Tree stands tall. It breathes and draws nutrients from the earth, to which it is deeply rooted.

The Body stands tall, breathes, and is fed by the earth. And, like the Tree, it is borne of this earth.

Look outside and notice a Tree. It is likely to be standing tall, its leaves flowing in the breeze, as it is warmed by the Sun. Now, look inside, and notice your body.

Often the posture slumps. When it does, oxygen flow can become compromised as the Breath becomes shallow. The Body tenses and mood can be impaired.

Assuming a posture that is upright and stable, like the Tree, can bring about a meaningful shift in mind and body. So too does observing the sensations arising in the body.

The Wind

The Wind represents the Breath.

When the Wind blows, it flows across the Earth, cooling, warming, cleansing, and oxygenating all of life.

The Breath arises in you, warming, cleansing, and oxygenating the Body.

While you can breathe on purpose, the Breath arises on its own. It happens naturally. When the Breath flows easily in and out, you feel relaxed, alert, and engaged. At times, things get in the way and inhibit the smooth flow of the Breath.

For example, when you have worrisome thoughts or are feeling emotionally agitated, the Breath becomes shallow, fast, and irregular, and a series of unpleasant sensations take hold of the Body.

Bringing awareness to the Breath can bring about a profound shift in your mental and physical well-being.

Clouds

Clouds represent Thoughts and Feelings.

Clouds cross the sky all day long. They change. They come and they go.

Thoughts and Feelings arise all day long. They change. They come and they go.

For example, look outdoors. If it is daytime, you probably notice Clouds. Now, look inside, into the activity of your mind. Do you notice Thoughts? Do you notice Feelings?

Something very important happens when you deliberately attend to the activity of the mind, and you notice the arising of Thoughts and Feelings.

This is especially so when you appreciate that the Thoughts and Feelings arising in this moment are soon to pass. Just like Clouds.

The Sun

The Sun represents Awareness, and the Warmth that nurtures the world.

When the Sun rises, it illuminates the world, effortlessly. Its warming rays flow without judgment, in all directions.

Awareness is a quality you possess, and it too arises effortlessly.

For example, reflect on a time when you were outside and drawn to a beautiful flower. This happened naturally. There was no trying, no judgment.

When we awaken to Awareness, we feel alive, fresh, and focused.

At times, things get in the way and obscure the fullness of our experience. For example, if you were lost in thought or were feeling very agitated, you probably would have missed seeing the flower.

Below is a recap of each Element and what it represents. Take a few moments and reflect on your connection to each Element.

Can you see aspects of yourself in each Element? Can you recognize the Element in yourself?

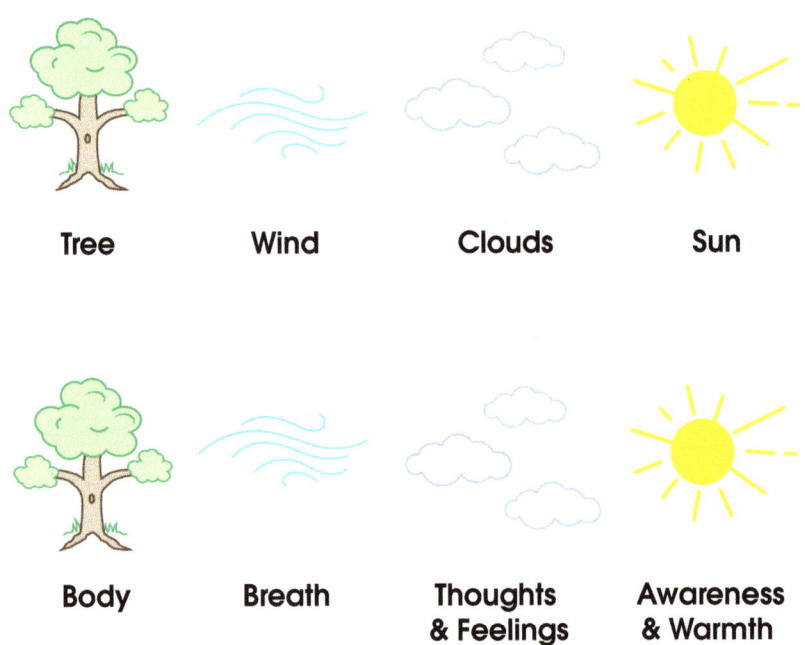

The next chapter explores this further and teaches you exercises associated with each Element. These exercises will help you "wake up," as you will encounter the Elements practically everywhere.

Inside and Outside

The Elements offer you an invitation to "wake up" out of automatic, mindless, and distracted states.

You know these states only too well. The great challenge is that when we are on automatic pilot and lost in thought, it can be very challenging to see the way out, because it is difficult to realize we are lost in the first place.

As you'll come to know from your direct experience, the deeper your connection to the Elements, the more readily they will serve as a "wake-up" call. The exercises in the next chapter teach you ways of connecting more deeply to the Elements.

But first, let's take a few moments and reflect a little more on the Elements and what they represent—on the inside and the outside.

On the Inside

Inside can mean indoors, in your home or office. Perhaps there is a potted tree or plant. The atmosphere may be conditioned by an AC unit or another source of airflow. The room is lighted overhead or by a lamp. And there are sounds, aromas, people, and pets, all coming and going.

Perhaps you can visualize this in your imagination, or observe it with your senses.

Inside can also mean inside of you. After all, you have a body, you breathe, you have thoughts and feelings, and you know this.

Below this is brought into sharper relief.

> Imagine you are watching a movie, captivated by the characters and storyline.
>
> You are sitting in a chair, your *body* tense, and, as the action intensifies, your *breathing* changes.
>
> *Emotions* pour through you as the plot takes its twists and turns. You're continually *thinking* about what is happening, its implications, and what may happen next.
>
> The movie ends, the lights are turned on, and you snap out of it and *realize* you were watching a movie.
>
> Look back over the above depiction and identify where the Tree, Wind, Clouds, and Sun are represented.

On the Outside

Outside can mean outdoors. After reading the next chapter, you will spend a little time outdoors observing the Elements in their natural state. They look something like this.

Outside can also mean outside of you. This may seem a little abstract at first, but in time it can become a profound insight.

To help this make a little more sense, below is a thought experiment.

> Imagine you are a fly on a wall observing yourself sitting in a room—perhaps as you are now.
>
> You are sitting and breathing, the air flowing in and out of your body.
>
> You are thinking, thoughts arising and passing through your mind. Feelings come and go.
>
> And, with the perspective of the fly, you are aware of this happening.
>
> Look at the above image. Can you see yourself sitting, breathing, thinking, and feeling? Aware of it all.

Chapter 2

Exploring the Elements: Doing

Something to Do

So that the Elements may begin to cue a shift to greater mindful awareness, we start with a simple exercise associated with each Element.

Each exercise takes but a second or two and invites you to "do" something when you see an Element.

You will find some of these exercises to be easy. Others may take a little practice. Exercises that involve Thoughts and Feelings tend to be the ones that call for a little more practice. This is because we can identify so closely with Thoughts and Feelings that we're not even aware we are having them.

Fundamental to mindfulness practice is developing this Awareness. To deepen this capacity, after you learn to "do" something when you see an Element in this chapter, the next chapter invites you to "be" present when you see an Element.

Together, these two exercises will deepen your understanding of the difference between "doing" and "being." You will begin to shift more readily between the two, thereby cultivating greater mindful awareness, moment by moment. This shift is known as the SoBe Mindful Flow.

When you see an image of a Tree,

ADJUST YOUR POSTURE

This adjustment is designed to bring about a more alert and engaged posture, as you may be slouching. It is not meant to be rigid; do not stick out your chest or lift your shoulders. You may keep your shoulders back and relaxed.

Poor posture constricts the Breath and can lead to chronic back, neck, and shoulder pain. This adjustment will also ready the Body for a more easeful flow of the Breath.

And because it is not always easy or necessary to adjust one's body posture, you can also extend and relax your fingers—like leaves on a branch.

When you see an image of the Wind,

TAKE A BREATH

Deliberately draw in and release a breath, breathing in through your nose and breathing out through your mouth (if comfortable). Breathe a little slower and deeper than your normal breath.

When you see an image of Clouds,

THINK A THOUGHT, FEEL A FEELING

It can be challenging to recognize thoughts and feelings—even to realize they are arising in the first place. In this exercise, you intentionally generate mental activity so that you will be sure not to miss it.

When you see a Cloud, turn your attention inward and think to yourself (word for word), "This is a Thought." Hear yourself saying these words in your mind.

Then, smile, as smiling tends to lift the mood, and think to yourself, "This is a Feeling." Pause long enough to feel the mood you've generated. Then frown, as frowning tends to drop the mood, and think, "This is a Feeling." As before, pause long enough to feel the mood you've generated.

Doing so, you will have generated Thoughts and Feelings, a powerful first step in learning to observe them at a distance—like clouds in the sky.

When you see an image of the Sun,

SPREAD WARMTH

Just as you breathe warmth into the world with every exhalation, so too can you offer kind wishes to yourself and another person.

When you see the sun or feel its warmth, bring to mind (or see before you) another person and offer them your warm regard by wishing them "May You Be Happy." Then wish for yourself, "May I Be Happy."

This exercise is not merely intellectual or abstract, as you are practicing cultivating a sincere wish for the kindness you are offering.

Beginning to Practice

The concluding pages to chapter 1 raise an important subject—the inside and outside aspects of the Elements.

The idea that you will find the Elements indoors (e.g., potted plant, AC, sounds, lamp) and outdoors (e.g., tree, winds, clouds, sun) is fairly straightforward.

But the idea that you will find the Elements inside and outside *of you* may be a little confusing. This is because we are not used to distinguishing between a thought we are having and a thought we are observing, or between a breath we are taking and a breath we are observing.

Most of the time—lost on automatic pilot—we are unaware of thinking and breathing because our mind is a million miles away and our body is being pulled along for the ride.

The short "doing" exercises you just learned begin the process of waking yourself up out of automatic pilot.

You can practice these exercises on the following pages when you see the Elements depicted. And you can do so, without the book, when you are outdoors.

Reinforcing the Elements

You have just learned instructions for your first set of SoBe Mindful exercises. These are important both as ends in themselves and because they are the building blocks of the SoBe Mindful Method.

So as to reinforce the practices associated with each Element, when you see an Element, recall the exercise and practice it.

You may find it helpful to name the Element and its association. The next page offers a visual to help you remember the associations for each Element.

A Short Practice

You are now ready to practice a short exercise.

You will guide yourself, cued by the imagery of the Elements contained on the pages of this book.

Slowly turn the following three pages and allow your gaze to fall on each of the selected images.

As you do, engage in the exercise associated with the Element.

The exercise should take around fifteen seconds. Proceed at a comfortable pace.

This short practice involved

1. Sitting upright.

2. Taking a breath.

3. Wishing "happiness" to another person and yourself.

Did you notice how the images spontaneously cued the instruction?

There was nothing to read. Nothing even to think.

Well done.

> Note: If it was challenging to remember what an Element cued, take a few moments and review the beginning of this chapter.

The Elements in the Natural World

This section reinforces what you just learned, setting the stage for bringing the practice outdoors, without needing the book.

Begin by reading this section while outdoors and follow the instructions, practicing with the Elements as you find them in nature.

When you notice a Tree,

adjust your posture so that it is more upright and stable.

Extend your fingers.

When you notice the Wind

(by feeling it against your skin or hearing it blow),

take a Breath.

Note: The SoBe Mindful Method invites you to take one breath. You may find it useful to take more than one breath. A common number of breaths taken at the beginning of many mindfulness practices is three.

When you notice a Cloud,

think the Thought "This is a Thought."

_____

Feel a Feeling by smiling and think,
"This is a Feeling," and by frowning, and
think, "This is a Feeling."

When you notice the Sun

(by feeling its warmth or
seeing it shine),

wish for another, "May You Be Happy,"
then wish for yourself, "May I Be Happy."

Now, close the book and take a walk.

As each Element reveals itself to you, practice the exercise you just learned.

Spend a little time doing this in a relaxed manner.

If you forget an association, open the book to this page, as the imagery below will serve as a helpful reminder.

Adjust the Posture **Think a Thought; Feel a Feeling**

Take a Breath **Spread Warmth**

Chapter 3

Exploring the Elements: Being

Shifting from Doing Mode to Being Mode

We now look to the Elements to cue a shift to "being" more fully present.

This is a useful exercise in and of itself, and it sets the stage for mastering the SoBe Mindful Method.

In the previous chapter you learned "doing" practices, which involve purposely making a change, be it adjusting the posture, softening your gaze, taking a breath, or intentionally generating a thought and feeling.

Each, in its own way, rouses us from automatic pilot. If our minds are wandering or distracted, we "wake up," even if only for a few moments.

In this chapter, the practice for each Element is one of "being," as opposed to "doing." These instructions also take but a second or two, and they invite you to "be" present with what is arising in the moment.

As a general matter, you can think of your actions as consisting of moments of "doing," where the objective is to bring something about, to make a change, and moments of "being," where you are allowing and noticing, but not trying to change anything.

This does not mean that change doesn't take place when you are "being" present. It simply means that it arises in a less effortful—a less needing-it-to-happen—way.

In order to make this shift from "doing" to "being," one of the Elements plays a pivotal role.

Can you think of which Element it is?

The Sun cues something very important as we move from doing to being.

As you know, the Sun represents Awareness. In the pages that follow, the Sun is paired with other Elements.

These pairings invite you to bring Awareness to the Element.

There is nothing to do. You do not adjust your posture (though that might happen spontaneously).

You do not take a Breath, nor do you think a Thought or feel a Feeling—though these may happen.

Instead, you observe the Breath. You observe the Body. You observe the arising of Thoughts and Feelings.

Truly, there is nothing to "do." Everything is happening on its own.

Believe it or not, sometimes nothing needs to be done—even when you think or feel certain that it does.

When you see an image of the Sun,

**NOTICE WHAT IS ARISING
IN THE FIELD OF AWARENESS**

It is common, especially when stressed, to narrow the field of vision—along with other sensory experiences.

This practice is one of opening to the larger landscape of what is before you—a wide-lens perspective.

No preference or agenda. Just looking. You may even notice a natural turning of the head to get a more complete view.

When you see an image of a Tree
and the Sun,

OBSERVE THE SENSATIONS
ARISING IN YOUR BODY

You may find it helpful to notice the sensations arising in and around your hands.

When you see an image of
the Wind and Sun,

**OBSERVE THE BREATHING THAT
IS HAPPENING**

When you see an image of Clouds and the Sun,

OBSERVE THE ARISING OF THOUGHTS AND FEELINGS

As with the "doing" exercise with Clouds, it can be challenging to observe Thoughts and Feelings, as sometimes we are not sure what we are thinking or feeling.

It is not necessary to come up with a response. What is most important is that you turn your attention to your interior experience and notice whatever you notice, whenever you notice it.

Through these exercises, you will appreciate that you are more than your Thoughts and Feelings. You learn from your direct experience that Thoughts and Feelings arise and pass away and that whatever part of them you "think" is you, doesn't last anyway.

The previous chapter noted that it can be confusing to think about finding the Elements inside and outside of you. This is because you may not be used to distinguishing between a thought you are having and a thought you are observing, or between a breath you are taking and a breath you are observing.

By observing the arising and passing away of thoughts, feelings, and sensations, it becomes clearer that what you previously may not have noticed at all, or took to be solid and fixed, was in fact a momentary experience—like the weather on a rainy day.

The "doing" exercises learned in the last chapter begin the process of waking up out of automatic pilot.

The "being" exercises explored in this chapter help you to remain awake, and through that sustained embrace of life's unfolding, to experience a greater sense of ease during challenging times. Even more, as you develop your capacity to remain mindful during life's challenging times, you more fully appreciate life's ebb and flow and deepen the cultivation of wisdom and compassion.

Reinforcing the Elements

You have just learned instructions for the second set of SoBe Mindful exercises—learning to "be" with the Elements.

So, to reinforce the practices associated with each Element, when you see an Element, recall the exercise and practice it.

You may find it helpful to name the Element and its association.

Please take your time as you turn these pages.

At this point in the last chapter, you were shown the image below with words and gestures as a reminder of what to do when you noticed an Element.

No words are needed when it comes to "being." We naturally know how to be present. It's a gentle turning inward—shining the light of awareness on our experience—and not "doing" anything. All that is needed is patience and curiosity.

Putting It All Together

Now, you will guide yourself, cued by the imagery of the paired Elements appearing on the following three pages.

Each page is its own short practice that engages the "being" aspect associated with the Elements.

Spend approximately ten to fifteen seconds on each, as it likely will take a few breaths to drop into the experience cued by the image.

Recognizing what the image depicts is not the practice. But recognizing it does help point the way to the more experiential "observational" stance intended by the image.

After sitting with each image for about ten to fifteen seconds, read the brief elaboration that follows.

Awareness of the Body

This exercise, fundamental to many mindfulness practices, invites you to direct your attention to the Body—more specifically, attending to the sensations arising in and around your body.

When you slow down and observe what is arising, moment by moment, you gather data—you notice things—that previously had gone unnoticed.

Tension, tightness, shallow breathing, an ache, an openness, an itch, a fullness, changing sensations, a tingling.

By being present and observing what is arising, without an agenda, you may naturally experience a shift in the activity of the Body, a subtle knowing; a gentle letting go.

Awareness of the Breath

This exercise offers you an important opportunity to more fully explore the Breath, moment by moment. The instruction is different from when the Wind appears by itself. When by itself, the Wind cues you to *take* a Breath.

This image cues you to bring attention to the Breath that is happening, and all that is called for is observing the Breath.

If you did not fully appreciate this when you saw the image, take a few moments now and observe the flow of air as it enters and leaves your body. There is nothing to do.

As you'll come to know from your direct experience, when you breathe with awareness of breathing, you become more mindfully aware.

You also become more skilled at noticing.

Awareness of Thoughts and Feelings

Many of us are not used to noticing what we are thinking or feeling. We often identify so closely with Thoughts and Feelings that it can be challenging to observe them. Instead, we become them. For example, when angry, our experience tends to be that we *are* angry as opposed to noticing that anger is arising. Sometimes, that can have consequences to our decision making and our well-being.

This exercise invites you to direct attention to your Thoughts and Feelings, and to notice what arises, changes, and passes away as you observe the coming and going of Thoughts and Feelings and other momentary fluctuations within the field of experience.

Rather than attending to something that seems "physical," like the Body or Breath, you are attending to something more subtle, almost abstract. But, as you'll learn, Thoughts and Feelings have more in common with the Breath and Body than you may "think."

As you become more aware of your Thoughts and Feelings, you begin to identify less strongly with them. Space emerges. You have more room to maneuver, to reflect, and to respond.

As you did before, close the book and take a walk outdoors in the sun.

As each Element reveals itself to you, practice the exercise you just learned.

Spend a little time being present in this manner. If you forget a pairing, open the book to this page, as the imagery below will serve as a helpful reminder.

Notice what is arising in the field of Awareness.

Observe Body sensations.

Observe the sensations of the Breath.

Observe Thoughts and Feelings.

Congratulations

By now, you should be familiar with each Element, whether you notice it on these pages or outdoors in nature.

You have been reinforcing what each Element represents and learned two short exercises to practice when you come across an Element, whether it is on these pages or outdoors.

One exercise involves "doing" and one involves "being." At any given moment you can observe what mode you are in. Much of the time you are on automatic pilot—not even knowing what mode you are in.

The two-step process of moving from "doing" to "being" in connection with an Element is known as the SoBe Mindful Flow. You'll return to it when you learn the mindfulness exercises in chapter 5.

Before we move on and you meet the Secondary Elements, it is worthwhile spending a little time exploring more fully the Breath, as it plays a fundamentally important role in mindfulness practice and in the SoBe Mindful Method.

A Tale of Two Breaths

The Breath has played a fundamental role in meditative practices for thousands of years.

One reason is because of the connection between mind and body. When the mind becomes agitated, the body follows. So too, as breathing becomes more easeful, slow, and regular, an agitated mind settles.

The Breath is one of the few regulatory processes of the body that happens automatically and can be controlled. You likely are breathing now without conscious effort and, if you choose, you can speed up or slow down the Breath. A variety of relaxation practices involve this deliberate manipulation of the Breath.

In contrast, mindfulness practice involves observing the Breath but not manipulating it. It is an exercise in allowing the moment to be as it is.

Doing so, you relate to what is arising from a place of wisdom and compassion—not resistance—and are better equipped to take, or not take, action to be responsive to the call of the moment.

The Breath is often regarded as a bridge between mind and body and plays a prominent role in many forms of meditation.

The Breath also exerts a powerful influence, regulating mental and physical processes associated with health and well-being. We all know what it is to breathe and are intimately familiar with the flow of air into and out of the body—the in-breath and the out-breath.

Now we'll explore the in-breath and out-breath from two overlapping perspectives so as to enrich your understanding of mindfulness and application of the SoBe Mindful Method.

The primary consideration involves the "taking" of a breath as opposed to "observing" a breath, a distinction to which you have already been introduced. You will also learn about the difference between a relaxation and a mindfulness practice.

A Few Tips on Breathing

A great deal has been written on optimal breathing. Posture, pacing, and muscular engagement all play a role in patterns of breathing that are healthy or can compromise well-being.

The breath you take is influenced by your posture. When the body is hunched and the posture slouched, the natural flow of the Breath is disrupted.

For this reason you will see that the SoBe Mindful Method explicitly addresses the posture most every time the Breath is engaged. This is done through imagery of the Tree, which cues an attentiveness to the posture and the sensations of the body.

Below are two rules of thumb for your posture and breathing.

Posture
When you are instructed to assume a posture that is upright and stable, attend to the quality of your posture such that it is comfortable and balanced. You are neither taking a rigid stance, nor one that is overly relaxed. A subtle adjustment may be all that is needed.

Breath
When you are instructed to take a breath, allow the belly to move with the breath. This will help ensure that breathing is not vertical (i.e., the up-and-down straining of the chest and shoulders), but horizontal (i.e., an expansion and contraction of the diaphragm). Deliberately slow down, drawing in air by expanding the diaphragm and using the same musculature to gently and fully expel air from your body.

If comfortable, breathe in through the nose and out through the mouth, as if blowing through a straw. Most important is breathing in a manner that is comfortable.

The spontaneous breath is the breath that is arising when you are not paying it any mind—it is the breathing that is happening most of the time.

As you are learning, at any moment, you can override the spontaneous breath by slowing down or speeding up your breathing.

Sometimes this can be helpful, as it can wake you up from "automatic pilot," and it can offer relief when breathing is erratic and you are feeling overwhelmed.

Sometimes, though, it can feel like a struggle, as if you are resisting your body's rhythm.

The exercises in this section will help you refine the ways you engage the Breath. This offers you greater mastery over using the Breath to achieve different states, such as relaxation.

You will also learn the value of observing, and not influencing, the natural rhythm of the Breath. This is part of the mindfulness journey, and a central aspect of many mindfulness practices.

In the pages that follow, take a slow, deep, comfortable breath each time you see the Wind Element. Be attentive to your posture.

There is no rush and no need to hurry through this exercise.

As noted before, if comfortable, breathe in through the nose and out through the mouth, as if blowing through a straw.

Thus far, the Wind has been the only Element involved in these guided exercises.

The mindfulness practice is more about "observing" than it is about "influencing" or "controlling."

This is where a relaxation practice and a mindfulness practice begin to part ways—though as the title to this chapter conveys, there is really but one breath, one moment. It is really a difference in how we are relating to the Breath. For indeed, were you to observe your breath throughout the day, you would notice hundreds, if not thousands, of different patterns of breathing.

As a concept, however, we can think of "taking" a breath as different from "observing" a breath. And indeed, we experience these two states differently.

When the Wind appears with the Sun, you notice the Breath moving through your body.

You direct your attention to the Breath and observe the bodily sensations of:

air flowing into and out of your nose or mouth, or

the movement of the belly,

or any other area where you connect to the Breath.

In the pages that follow, observe the bodily sensations of breathing each time you see a pairing of the Sun and Wind Elements.

When there is no pairing, take a breath.

Do You Notice The Difference?

With the Sun, you are observing. There is no effort, no need to try to breathe. You're becoming more aware of what is happening.

Without the Sun, breathing is on purpose, deliberate.

> Sometimes, taking a series of slow, deep, quiet, and regular breaths can bring about a sense of calm.
>
> This is in the service of relaxation.

> Sometimes, attending to the sensations of the Breath also brings about a sense of calm. Achieving a relaxed state is not a primary objective of mindfulness practice.
>
> Mindfulness practice is in the service of the cultivation of awareness—of wisdom and compassion.

The deliberate manipulation of the Breath helps brings about a shift in body regulation—a shift from sympathetic (fight/flight) to parasympathetic (relaxation) nervous system arousal.

In contrast, observing the sensations of breathing is an end in itself. It may tone down the busyness of the mind. For rather than feeding the frenzy of thinking (of past and future and the emotional toll it can take), attention is directed to the body. It's like you stop throwing rocks into a lake; the water settles because it is no longer being agitated. Nothing is being done to the water to make it settle.

This distinction is important.

To help you more fully connect with the difference, follow the guided practices on the following pages.

Are you able to observe two breaths without feeling like you are *trying* to breathe?

The key is the realization that breathing is happening, whether you try or not.

If it feels labored, stop trying to breathe, and wait for breathing to arise on its own.

By now you are probably acquiring a more-nuanced appreciation for what it means to take a breath as opposed to observing a breath you are taking.

You probably are also experiencing the mental and physical shift that is involved.

It takes practice to shift comfortably between these two states.

It also takes practice to observe the Breath for more than a few moments without slipping into controlling the Breath, or getting lost in distraction.

Come back to this section from time to time to practice shifting from *taking* to *observing* the Breath.

And, of course, you can do this anytime. When you are outdoors and you feel the breeze, that can be a reminder to practice, first by taking a few breaths, and then shifting to observing a few breaths.

Chapter 4

The Secondary Elements

The Secondary Elements

The four Primary Elements are central to the SoBe Mindful invitation, and almost all of the mindfulness exercises you will learn draw upon them.

There are two additional Elements that are also very important. They are referred to as Secondary Elements and are explored in this chapter.

You will find that they enrich your practice—perhaps in a transformative way—as they connect to fundamentally important insights and ways of cultivating and sustaining presence.

A Bird

A Butterfly

What the Secondary Elements Represent

A Bird = Listening

A Butterfly = Gratitude

Mindfulness Insights and the Secondary Elements

As with the Primary Elements, each of the Secondary Elements also represents an important aspect of mindfulness practice.

A Bird

A Bird represents Listening.

When a bird is nearby, it is common to hear its song.

A natural response to birdsong is to listen—listen with delight.

Reflect on hearing birds chirping in the early morning, or when you are out in nature.

Hearing birdsong is often a delightful, even treasured, experience. The song awakens us naturally to the beauty of its sound.

Importantly, we are not trying to listen. We are not trying to figure out what the bird is saying—as that would only get in the way.

We simply wake up to the arising of sound.

A Butterfly

A Butterfly represents Gratitude.

Just as a caterpillar matures into a Butterfly, so too do we transform as we journey through life.

We appreciate that there is so much for which to be grateful, and, at the same time, we forget.

The Butterfly is delicate, as is our precious life and the lives of all beings.

We take delight as it flits about among flowers, trees, rivers, unbounded and expansive in its journey.

Grateful to be alive, liberated, and free.

All that it touches can awaken us to the bounty of our lives and our many blessings.

Review:
Remembering the Elements

The following page depicts each of the Secondary Elements.

For each one, name the Element and what it represents.

Name the Element

What Does the Element Represent?

Answers are on the next page.

 Listening

 Gratitude

Now, close your eyes and bring to mind each of the Secondary Elements.

As you do, recall what they represent.

If you forget, open your eyes and remind yourself.

Element-Inspired Practice

As with the Primary Elements, there is a simple practice that is associated with each Secondary Element.

These Elements also naturally cue a shift to greater mindful awareness.

There is one difference worth noting at the outset between the Primary and Secondary Elements. Whereas the Primary Elements invite both a *doing* and a *being* mode, the Secondary Elements tend to spontaneously cue the *being* mode.

When you see an image of a Bird,

LISTEN

The Listening faculty tends to arise naturally, without effort.

When you see an image of a Butterfly,

SPARK GRATITUDE

Gratitude is not something we create or manufacture. Rather, it involves bringing to mind something for which we are already grateful—that we've momentarily forgotten about. Doing so, positive feelings surface and can be more fully felt and cultivated.

The term "spark" is intended to connect to the reality that we are bringing something more fully to life.

To spark Gratitude is to awaken a felt sense of Gratitude.

A Short Practice

So that you may have a sense of the interplay between the Primary and Secondary Elements, you will now guide yourself, cued by the imagery appearing on the following three pages.

Slowly turn each page and allow your gaze to rest on each image.

As you do, engage in the exercise associated with the Element and its pairing. This exercise calls on you to apply what you have been learning to pairings that are new to you.

The exercise should take around twenty to thirty seconds.

Proceed at a comfortable pace.

Were you able to remember what each Element represented, and the practice associated with it?

Upon seeing the Tree, you adjusted your posture.

With the introduction of the Wind, you took a breath.

The image of the Sun and Wind introduced the pairing of two Elements.

What did you do when you saw this pairing?

The image invited you to observe the arising of two in-breaths and out-breaths.

The Butterfly and Wind Elements invited you to bring a sense of Gratitude for the Breath.

You can do this in many ways, personal to you. The essence of the practice is to feel a sense of Gratitude for being alive—for the gift of the Breath.

A Word about Listening

Just as we are always breathing, we are always listening. And just as we can breathe without awareness, we can listen without awareness. Often we are listening to the voice in our head.

It's as if we are listening to our thoughts, passively accepting what we are hearing, unaware that we have a choice—that there is more.

To listen with Awareness is to become open and receptive to the arising of sound. It's Listening, as if with ears that are hearing for the first time.

It can be helpful to lower or close the eyes when practicing Listening, as this helps tone down distraction, and sharpen the Listening faculty.

The image of the Bird appears on the next page with a set of closed eyes. They invite you to close or lower your eyes as you attend to the sounds arising in your midst.

Let's practice a few more pairings.

In time, as you become familiar practicing with the Elements, you may wish to modify the practices so that they resonate especially well with you.

Grateful for the Body.

Listening to the Breath.

A Word about Gratitude

Many of us come across butterflies only on occasion. It is not necessary to actually see one to spark Gratitude.

A common setting that can readily cue imagery of a butterfly is a patch of flowers. This is because we naturally tend to associate butterflies and flowers.

Part II

Practice

Chapter 5

The SoBe Mindful Flow and Punctuated Practice

Now that you are familiar with the SoBe Mindful Method, you likely will begin to spontaneously wake up out of automatic pilot at various moments during the day, cued by the Elements.

I have termed this spontaneous emergence of greater mindful awareness *punctuated mindfulness,* and the practicing of mindfulness during these moments, *punctuated practice.* This is in contrast to mindfulness practices that are planned, or more formal.

In the next chapter you'll learn the SoBe Mindful Flow, which is a building block of many punctuated practices. As you may already have come to appreciate, the SoBe Mindful Method offers you the freedom to play with and relate to the Elements in ways that resonate with you, to enrich your understanding and practice of mindfulness.

Punctuated Practice

Punctuated practice refers to practice that accompanies the spontaneous emergence of mindful awareness throughout the day. It adds depth and richness to these moments and reinforces their emergence. The practice of mindfulness, as a general matter, tends to facilitate periods of heightened awareness, of "waking up." Such moments often are short-lived, yet can be meaningful and heartfelt, and present opportunities to see more clearly, and be more responsive to, what is arising in the present moment.

As you have no doubt noticed, expansive moments of alertness—of waking up—are sooner or later met with a contraction, a falling asleep. Focus . . . distracted. Alert . . . groggy. Engaged . . . detached. Moving back and forth between these states has become a habit. But it's in our nature, when conditions ripen, to wake up, and to stay awake.

Punctuated mindfulness helps us connect more deeply with the loving embrace and steadiness of the present moment. Recall a time you saw a sunset, a waterfall, a flower, or the vastness of the ocean or a mountain range and were stopped in your tracks. You didn't think your way into it; it just happened.

You may also recollect moments when you were feeling agitated and uneasy. You may have been alone and lost in worrisome or judgmental thoughts, or perhaps you were interacting with someone in a difficult encounter. And then, something happened and you woke up; for a flicker of an instant you glimpsed that the stance you were taking was reactive, defensive, and not helpful, or that the other person was suffering, struggling.

Moments such as these offer a brief window of opportunity to step out of reactivity and remain mindfully aware a little longer.

The SoBe Mindful Stop and SoBe Mindful Minute are two punctuated practices that you can draw upon amid these windows of opportunity. They insert a wedge of awareness into your experience, thereby increasing the likelihood that you sustain a mindful state—or temper a reactive one. Central to these practices is the *doing-to-being* shift you learned for each Element. This movement from *doing* to *being* is known as the SoBe Mindful Flow and is discussed more fully, and applied to everyday circumstances, in the pages that follow.

The SoBe Mindful Flow

The SoBe Mindful Flow ("the Flow") involves connecting with the Elements to awaken more fully into present-moment Awareness.

We spend a lot of time lost in our thoughts—ruminating about the past, narrating the present, and anticipating the future. During such times, we can be on automatic pilot. Waking up out of automatic pilot sets the stage for the SoBe Mindful Flow—the transition from a state *conditioned* by prior experience to one *receptive* to the unfolding of experience. The question is, what do we "do" after waking up from automatic pilot?

> **Automatic Pilot** —> Doing —> Being

While it is not necessary to follow the linear path depicted above, a helpful place to start is by *doing* something, and this you learned when you first met the Elements. For example, *doing* something might involve assuming an upright posture (Tree) or taking a breath (Wind). Then, after becoming grounded in *doing*, you shift into *being*.

In reality, *doing* and *being* are always at play, but the heaviness that can accompany the habitual, often defensive and reactive states we find ourselves in, can get in the way.

The following offers you an example of how to move along this path.

Imagine you are outside walking, on your way to meet someone. For the past few days you've been worrying about test results you'll be receiving soon. You don't realize it, but you're in a fretful state. Your thoughts are lost in worst-case scenarios, you're feeling anxious, your breathing is shallow, your body is rigid, and you're barely aware of what's taking place around you.

Then, for any of a variety of reasons, you momentarily wake up out of this uncomfortable state. It could be because the discomfort got to be too much, or that you are distracted by a sound or event happening around you. Your phone may have vibrated, or maybe, owing to practicing the SoBe Mindful Method, you "feel" the Wind and "wake up."

Whatever the reason, you have snapped out of it, and you perceive the moment with greater clarity. Aware that you have been on automatic pilot, you are interested in staying awake and so you turn to the Elements. At this moment, let us say that the Wind is most salient, so you shift into *doing* with the Wind by *taking a breath*.

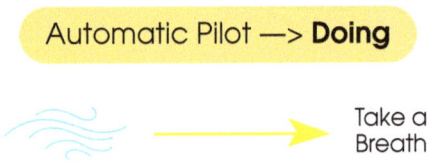

After taking a breath—or perhaps a few—you shift into *being* by observing the Breath.

The Flow is depicted for each of the Primary Elements. Importantly, the Flow is directed to the Primary (as opposed to Secondary) Elements because each has an explicit "doing" and "being" component. The Secondary Elements are a little different in that they more immediately engage "being."

The SoBe Mindful Flow: Doing to Being

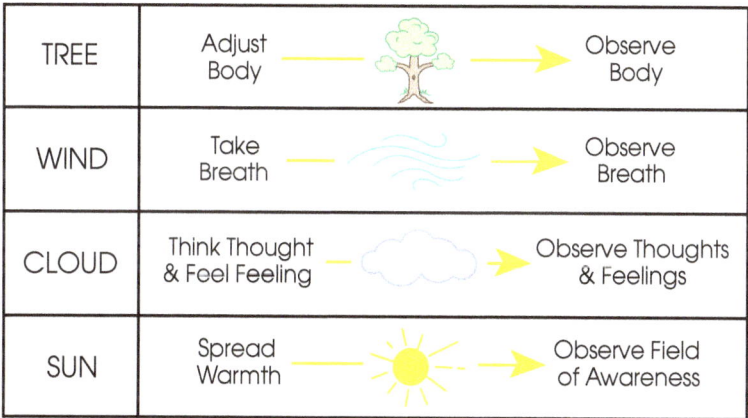

TREE	Adjust Body	→	Observe Body
WIND	Take Breath	→	Observe Breath
CLOUD	Think Thought & Feel Feeling	→	Observe Thoughts & Feelings
SUN	Spread Warmth	→	Observe Field of Awareness

Practice the SoBe Mindful Flow with each of the Elements and see if one resonates more with you than the others. If so, this may be your "GoTo" Element.

The Breath plays a central role in the SoBe Mindful Method. Because practicing with the Wind incorporates the Breath, when you are practicing the Flow with one of the other Elements, you may find it helpful for the Breath to set the tempo, as you move from *doing* to *being*.

The SoBe Mindful Stop

The SoBe Mindful Stop offers you an opportunity to slow down, wake up, and see a little more clearly what's taking place before you, and within you.

The practice inserts a purposeful pause into your experience, is simple and easy to remember, and can be based on any of the Elements.

As a punctuated practice, you can turn to it anytime and can practice it for as little or as long as you choose.

Practicing the SoBe Mindful Stop

The SoBe Mindful Stop is an accessible practice that you can turn to anytime, and may well do so multiple times a day. The only prerequisite to practice is that you wake up out of automatic pilot. This might be occasioned by something you are thinking, hearing, or seeing that rouses you into a heightened level of Awareness. Perhaps your thoughts are so agitating that something inside of you steps outside of its oppressive stream. Or maybe you are bored, or you become aware of something in the environment that snaps you out of a distracted or reactive state.

Whatever the cause, the SoBe Mindful Stop offers you an accessible and simple means of inserting a wedge of Awareness into your experience.

How to Practice

You need but a few seconds to practice. You may be in the middle of a conversation, working on a project, or about to walk into a meeting. This exercise builds directly off of the SoBe Mindful Flow as follows:

1. Come to a stop. (If you are unable to come to a complete stop, slow down your pace.)
2. Bring an Element to mind.
3. Practice the SoBe Mindful Flow with that Element.
4. Resume what you were doing.

The most common approach is to practice the SoBe Mindful Stop by selecting an Element and then moving from *doing* to *being*. Of course, you may instead choose to rest in *doing*, or skip *doing* and move directly into *being*. Often, the path you take will depend on your state of mind and body at the time. The busier the mind and more agitated the body, the greater the tendency to begin and linger with *doing*.

You will find this practice to be surprisingly effective and refreshing. Coming to a stop is itself a powerful practice. Coming to a stop and relaxing or becoming more attentive to what is arising in the field of Awareness can be clarifying and helpful. And, on those occasions when you are outdoors, the practice can be especially refreshing.

Choosing an Element

There are a variety of ways you may select the Element with which to practice. Some appear below. Some will naturally come to you.

—Having a "GoTo" Element at the ready. If one Element in particular resonates with you—for example, the Wind—select it as your "GoTo" Element.

—Drawing upon an Element that is most salient in the moment. If, for example, you are walking outside and your attention is drawn to the clouds, you may naturally turn to the Cloud Element.

—Selecting an Element that feels applicable under the circumstance. If feeling shaken by an event, you may turn to the Tree Element, as a symbol of stability. If angry with someone, you may turn to the Sun Element and spread Warmth. A chart is found on the next page.

> It can be helpful to identify your *GoTo* Element in advance so that when the time emerges, you can readily immerse in the practice. Consider which of the Elements you connect with the most and practice with it often.

Note that while the Bird and Butterfly Elements do not have as much of a *doing* aspect, they work well for this practice, especially if awakened by the sight or sound of a bird, or of a butterfly or flowers. You simply move directly into *being*.

Element Suggestions for Different Circumstances

STATE	ELEMENT	OBJECT
Scattered Confused Doubtful	(tree)	Body
Anxious Angry Scattered	(wind)	Breath
Judgmental Self-righteous Moody	(clouds)	Thoughts and Feelings
Sad Restless Angry	(sun)	Kindness and Awareness
Obsessing Despairing Tired	(bird)	Listening
Jealous Dejected Depressed	(butterfly)	Gratitude

SoBe Mindful Minute

The SoBe Mindful Minute is a short exercise you can practice anytime to both bring about a little calm and move into a more mindful state. It is easy to remember because it tracks the Elements, as you learned them. While you may lengthen it by resting for more than a single breath, or a few moments, with each Element, the practice takes about a minute.

While you can keep your eyes open, it is recommended that you close them, if convenient and comfortable to do so, to enrich the experience. One exception is if you are outside. You may draw upon the imagery you see and feel to guide you—and perhaps more fully engage the sensory aspects of the practice.

Practicing the SoBe Mindful Minute

The SoBe Mindful Minute involves practicing the SoBe Mindful Flow for each Element, beginning with the Tree. It is helpful, when outdoors, to direct your attention to each Element or, when indoors, to imagine or visualize each Element as you do so. The exercise is depicted below.

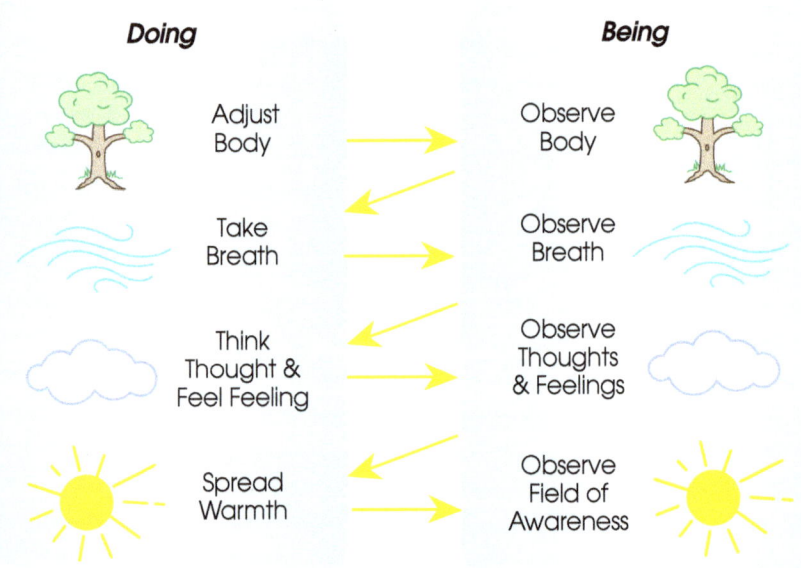

As you finish this practice, you may be naturally inclined to incorporate one or both of the Secondary Elements. For example, the expanded field of Awareness occasioned by the Sun may lead to your bringing to mind the Bird Element and prompt you to listen to what is arising in the soundscape. Or, perhaps the Butterfly Element comes to mind and you reflect on something for which you are grateful.

Practice Suggestions for Different Circumstances

The SoBe Mindful Minute can be helpful to insert a wedge of Awareness in the midst of a challenging or uneasy situation.

Drawing on Viktor Frankl's insight that "between stimulus and response there is a space, and within that space is the power to choose our response," deliberately pausing between an event and a possible (over)reaction enlarges the space to choose a more intentional and useful response. Importantly, the space is supported and enriched through the deliberate mindfulness practice inherent in the SoBe Mindful Minute.

Examples of instances where practice can be helpful include:

1. After receiving an undesirable e-mail and before replying.
2. When becoming angry in a conversation.
3. When you feel an impulse to eat food that you would rather avoid.
4. When standing in line and feeling restless or bored.

Frequently, the decision to draw upon the exercise follows an appreciation of the disconnect between intention and inclination. Even if a few moments after beginning the exercise, or upon completing it, you engage in conduct you had hoped to avoid, still you will have begun the process of more skillfully attending to that challenging moment. In time, you will likely come to realize a meaningful shift taking place in which you feel greater mastery over your thoughts and actions.

The SoBe Mindful Now

The SoBe Mindful Now refers to a state of present-moment Awareness. It is more an immersion in experience than a practice, and the word "now" is a place to be rather than a pointer for when to get there.

It can be helpful to think of losing yourself in the richness of the present moment, by "flowing with, or becoming one with, the Elements." And, as we've been exploring, the walls of separation between Tree and Body, Wind and Breath, Clouds and Thoughts/Feelings, and the Sun and Awareness are perhaps more illusory than real. Our true nature is *nature*, and the natural world can be our guide to finding our way back home.

The SoBe Mindful Stop and SoBe Mindful Minute, along with other mindfulness practices, help establish a readiness to experience the SoBe Mindful Now. But, unlike discussion of the SoBe Mindful Stop and the SoBe Mindful Minute, discussing the SoBe Mindful Now only gets us so far, as it is the practicing of mindfulness that opens the doorway.

Flowing with the Elements

Living a mindful life does not require effortful practice. The two short exercises you just learned, the SoBe Mindful Stop and SoBe Mindful Minute, are practiced to deepen your connection to the present moment, with the SoBe Mindful Flow inviting a deliberate transitioning from *doing* to *being* to facilitate this shift. The beauty of turning to the Elements as a form of practice is that you are *re-turning* to nature, and to your true nature.

Sometimes you will find that as you flow from *doing* to *being* you naturally let go of *being* as a conscious endeavor and experience an open and receptive state of presence. We call this "Flowing with the Elements." You are the Tree, your Breath is the Wind, your mind is the Clouds, and you are aware.

You may also find—especially if you are an experienced practitioner—that you begin "Flowing with the Elements" even without engaging the two-part process. You may, for example, notice an Element and shift to a state of *being* (i.e., you feel the Wind and become aware of the Breath)—and then spontaneously fall into the moment. Or perhaps there is no deliberate attention paid to the Elements, and no purposeful engagement with *doing* or *being*. Rather, you connect with an Element and spontaneously awaken. This would be akin to my experience driving down US-1 and seeing the tree.

You likely wil experience this more often when you are outside, communing with nature. You may already know this from your direct experience. And because the Elements are also found inside, there is no place in particular you have to be to spontaneously awaken. In all cases, you *awaken from within*.

One way to engage in the deeper experience of "Flowing with the Elements" when you are outside is to come to a physical standstill as you are practicing the SoBe Mindful

Stop or SoBe Mindful Minute. A flexible aspect of these practices is that you can be in motion while practicing. Coming to a standstill—to literally stop in your tracks—can lead to a powerful experience, even if but for a few glorious moments.

The movement from *doing* to *being* that informs much of the SoBe Mindful Method now drops to a deeper level. In the words of beloved mindfulness teacher and Zen master, Thich Nhat Hanh, you move into a state of *interbeing*, where there is an abiding sense that all is connected, that everything owes its existence to everything else.

Drawing on the linear construction previously set forth, you can think of it as moving from:

> automatic pilot —> doing —> being —> **interbeing**

While as a practice and learning tool this linear depiction can be helpful to understanding and monitoring these shifts, there is nothing inherently linear about the Flow.

> Conceptually, we locate ourselves on the above continuum, and this mapping is helpful to the "thinking mind" to know where we are "on the path." The challenge is that we keep trying to know where we are and to get somewhere else (better), when in fact we are already here, we are already awake, and it is always now. We just keep forgetting.

Chapter 6

Planned Practices

Planned Practices

It is helpful to practice mindfulness on a regular basis. A good rule of thumb is to practice daily for an amount of time that is agreeable to you, given your daily schedule.

Traditionally daily practice might last for anywhere between twenty and ninety minutes, once or twice a day. With a growing number of people from all walks of life becoming interested in mindfulness, suggested daily practice time has dropped, with research supporting the efficacy of shorter practice time. My colleague, the cognitive neuroscientist Amishi Jha, finds that measurable benefits may accompany twelve minutes of practice. Some prominent teachers suggest that short practices, engaged many times a day, can also be very helpful. And practically all agree some is better than none.

In this section you will learn three planned practices: the SoBe Mindful Sunrise, the SoBe Mindful & Kind, and the SoBe Mindful & Grateful. As planned practices, you can designate a set time in the day to practice them. For example, when you wake up in the morning, you can practice the SoBe Mindful Sunrise. You can practice SoBe Mindful & Kind during a break in the day, perhaps before or after lunch. These can become pleasant rituals that wake you up—even after you thought you had already woken up when you got out of bed.

Because planned practices involve sitting for longer than a few breaths, the mind is more likely to wander. The SoBe Mindful Method offers useful imagery to draw upon during mind wandering, along with traditional mindfulness instruction for skillfully responding when it does.

A Word About the Wandering Mind

It is normal to be distracted while practicing mindfulness. Realizing this firsthand can be illuminating ("Is my attention really that fragile?") and inspire practice.

SoBe Mindful imagery for the distracted mind is the Sun being blocked by a Cloud.

Of course, the Sun has not gone anywhere. This is a natural happening, one that you've observed many times. It's just that during these times, the Sun has become temporarily hidden behind a Cloud.

Temporary, because Clouds move on. They accumulate and dissipate. It is helpful to remember that when this happens, the Cloud does not need to go away, for awareness is large enough to hold everything, even the Cloud.

It is helpful to regard mind wandering as a natural and temporary state.

Practicing Mindfulness

When you realize that your mind has wandered and you have become distracted from the object on which you had initially placed your attention, (e.g., Body, Breath, Thoughts), gently escort your attention back to the object on which it had been resting. This calls for little if any effort—it is the natural *remembering* of where you were a few moments before you drifted off.

SoBe Mindful Sunrise

The SoBe Mindful Sunrise is a beautiful practice for starting the day. The metaphor of the sun rising reminds us that we can "wake up" anytime, even in the middle of the day.

The practice appears on the following pages as a book-guided practice with instructions. This means that you can use the book to guide practice, much as you would an audio recording. After a short period of time, you will be able to practice it by memory.

The practice begins just before dawn, when attention is directed to the Elements, one by one. Then, as dawn breaks and the Sun emerges, you observe the Elements, one by one. During the *being* phase you can settle into a traditional mindfulness practice, be it oriented around the body, breath, mind, or an expanded field of awareness.

A Tree Stands Before Dawn

Bring yourself into a posture that is upright and stable.

(If reclining, you may wish to instead stretch and relax your body/hands.)

The Wind Blows Before Dawn

Take a slow, deep breath.

The Clouds Overhead Before Dawn

Think a Thought; feel a Feeling.

Dawn Breaks

Spread Warmth

(Bring to mind another person and wish them the kindness "May You Be Happy." Then wish this kindness to yourself, "May I Be Happy.")

**The Sun Begins to Rise
and Shines on a Tree**

Observe Body sensations.

*You may choose to settle into this phase and practice either a body awareness or a body scan practice. See pages 182–183 for more information.

The Sun Shines on the Wind

Observe the Breath.

*You may choose to settle into this phase and practice a breath awareness practice. See pages 182–183 for more information.

The Sun Shines on the Clouds

Observe Thoughts and Feelings.

*You may choose to settle into this step and practice what is known as a labeling practice. See pages 182-183 for more information.

The Sun Is Shining

Expand the field of Awareness.
(Open your eyes / lift your gaze.)

*You may choose to settle into this step and practice what is known as a bare attention or open monitoring practice. See pages 182-183 for more information.

SoBe Mindful Sunrise Review

After moving through the *doing* phase for each Element, you can rest your attention, for the remainder of the practice, on any of the Elements and practice a fundamental mindfulness exercise.

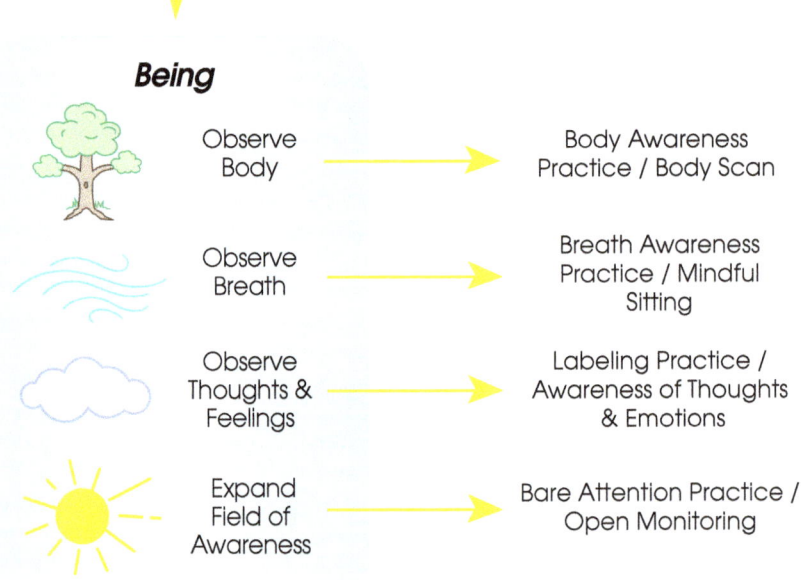

If you are familiar with one or more of these practices, you will readily intuit how they dovetail with the SoBe Mindful Sunrise. If these are new to you, you will find helpful pointers on the next page. The list of resources, found on page 210, will provide you with information and insights for deepening your understanding of these practices.

You may already be familiar with one or more of the below practices and, as previously discussed, you can integrate them into the SoBe Mindful Sunrise. If they are new to you, you can begin to practice with the brief instruction below, and are encouraged to learn with a teacher, a group, or through another form of instruction, support, and guidance.

Body Awareness involves resting attention on the sensations arising within the body, observing them arise, change, and pass away.

Body Scan involves resting attention on an area of the body and observing sensations, noting whether they are pleasant, unpleasant, or neutral. The entire body is slowly scanned in this way, moving from the toes to the head. Often, it is practiced while lying down.

Breath Awareness involves focusing attention on the Breath, attending to the flow of air as it moves into and out of the body.

Labeling / Awareness of Thoughts and Feelings involves resting attention on the Breath and, upon noticing that your mind has wandered, noting silently "thought," "feeling" (or "sensation").

Bare Attention / Open Monitoring involves observing and sustaining nonjudgmental attention on whatever arises in and passes through the field of awareness.

For the first three practices, when you notice your mind wandering, gently return attention to the Breath and continue the practice. For the Bare Attention practice, this is a helpful instruction when you realize an expanded field of awareness has collapsed and your thoughts are elsewhere.

The SoBe Mindful Minute as a Planned Practice

You may have noticed that the SoBe Mindful Minute and the SoBe Mindful Sunrise are similar with the exception that the SoBe Mindful Minute flows from *doing* to *being* for each Element, whereas the SoBe Mindful Minute flows first through the *doing* for each Element, and then through *being*.

As a punctuated practice, the Flow between *doing* and *being* inherent in the SoBe Mindful Minute is helpful, for even if you stop along the way, you will have had the opportunity to practice both *doing* and *being*. Because it is a short exercise that lends itself nicely to being practiced outdoors, the movement from *doing* to *being* may, from time to time, lead to a state of *interbeing* (see page 167), as you begin Flowing with the Elements.

This said, it may well be the case that you find the flow of the SoBe Mindful Minute helps to establish a meaningful planned practice. As such, you may choose to flow from *doing* to *being* for each Element and then, when you get to the Sun, you drop into a period of mindfulness practice.

Whatever approach you take, the primary takeaway is that the SoBe Mindful Method is a flexible approach that you can adapt in ways that resonate with you. Because the method draws upon fundamental elements of mindfulness practice, your personalized treatment likely will hold the integrity of the practice.

SoBe Mindful & Kind

The SoBe Mindful & Kind practice cultivates kind regard for yourself and others in a manner that follows in the tradition of "lovingkindness" practice.

It tracks the SoBe Mindful Sunrise with a fuller expression of kindness practiced *as dawn breaks*. The *doing* practice of spreading Warmth is expanded to include the following:

May I Be Safe.
May I Be Happy.
May I Be Healthy.
May I Live with Ease of Heart.

The practice is offered to others in a deliberate manner such that you offer it to a benefactor, a neutral person, a challenging person, and to all beings.

A Tree Stands Before Dawn

Bring yourself into a posture that is upright and stable.

(If reclining, you may wish to instead stretch and relax your body/hands.)

The Wind Blows Before Dawn

Take a slow, deep breath.

The Clouds Overhead Before Dawn

Think a Thought; feel a Feeling.

Dawn Breaks

Spread Warmth with a gentle exhalation.

Spread Warmth to Yourself

(Bring to mind a sense of yourself, at this time in your life, and wish for yourself . . .)

May I Be Safe.
May I Be Happy.
May I Be Healthy.
May I Live with Ease of Heart.

Spread Warmth to a Benefactor

(Bring to mind someone who has been good to
you in this life and wish for that person . . .)

May You Be Safe.
May You Be Happy.
May You Be Healthy.
May You Live with Ease of Heart.

Spread Warmth to a Neutral Person

(Bring to mind someone for whom you do not have feelings, one way or the other, and wish for that person . . .)

May You Be Safe.
May You Be Happy.
May You Be Healthy.
May You Live with Ease of Heart.

Spread Warmth to a Difficult Person

(Bring to mind someone with whom you have a difficult relationship and wish for that person . . .)

May You Be Safe.
May You Be Happy.
May You Be Healthy.
May You Live with Ease of Heart.

Spread Warmth to All Beings

(Bring to mind a sense of all beings living in this world, including yourself, and wish . . .)

May All Beings Be Safe.
May All Beings Be Happy.
May All Beings Be Healthy.
May All Beings Live with Ease of Heart.

The Sun Begins to Rise and Shines on a Tree

Observe Body sensations.

The Sun Shines on the Wind

Observe the Breath.

The Sun Shines on the Clouds

Observe Thoughts and Feelings.

The Sun Is Shining

Expand the Field of Awareness.
(Open Your Eyes / lift Your gaze.)

Lovingkindness practices have a rich history across a variety of wisdom traditions. This exercise tracks one popularized by Sharon Salzberg and shared by many superb teachers.

By beginning with the *doing* practices of the Tree, Wind, and Clouds, you establish a foundation for practice, which unfolds through the spreading of Warmth with the Sun. Then, after cultivating lovingkindness, the exercise closes with the *being* practices associated with each of the Elements.

To learn more about lovingkindness, you can read Sharon Salzberg's books, *Lovingkindness, A Heart As Wide As the World, Real Happiness, The Kindness Handbook*, and *Real Love*.

SoBe Mindful & Grateful

The SoBe Mindful & Grateful practice involves the cultivation of gratitude and connection.

The imagery facilitates the expression of Gratitude toward yourself and another person, as you connect with a chosen Element within yourself, and within another person.

As with the other planned practices in this book, you can practice using the book, or you can remember the Flow and practice without a book.

This exercise is also one that can be readily and meaningfully practiced during the day when you see a Butterfly. As a punctuated practice, you may wish to bring to mind just one Element and practice for yourself and the person you bring to mind.

Grateful for the Body

Reflect on the marvel of having a body, and feel a sense of Gratitude for your body.

Bring to mind someone you care about and feel a sense of Gratitude that they have a body.

Grateful for the Breath

Reflect on the marvel of being able to breathe, and feel a sense of Gratitude for the Breath.

Bring to mind someone you care about and feel a sense of Gratitude that they are able to breathe.

Grateful for Thoughts and Feelings

Reflect on the gift of being able to think and feel, and cultivate a sense of Gratitude for being able to do so.

Bring to mind someone you care about and feel a sense of Gratitude that they are able to think and feel.

Grateful to be Aware

Reflect on the wonder of Awareness, and feel a sense of Gratitude that you are aware.

Bring to mind someone you care about and feel a sense of Gratitude that they are aware.

You may choose to replace Awareness with Warmth and cultivate Gratitude for being able to be feel warmth and kindness for others.

Answers to Common Questions

Q: Is there a reason why the SoBe Mindful Flow moves from *doing* to *being* and not the other way around?

A: The *doing* practice is intended to help steady the body and settle the mind by drawing attention inward. This establishes a more stable foundation for the engagement of greater mindful awareness.

Q: The doing practices for the Tree and Wind are pretty simple, whereas the *doing* practice for Clouds seems complicated. Is there a reason why? Is it important that I follow the instructions?

A: As a general rule, we tend to regard the Body and Breath as somewhat separate from "who we are." We think "I am breathing" and "I have a body." In contrast, we can so identify with thoughts that we regard them as "who we are." "I am my thoughts" is not an uncommon belief. So too with our feelings. Yet, we can be aware of Body, aware of Breath, and aware of Thoughts and Feelings as objects arising in consciousness. The *doing* practice for "Clouds" is intended to help allow a greater discernment of our Awareness of Thoughts and Feelings. By deliberately thinking "This is a thought," the thought becomes more apparent. You may further explore this by thinking "This is not a thought." Along with eliciting the realization that "thoughts are not facts," it can be a bit of a mind-bender. Similarly, the generation of a positive and negative feeling state with a smile and frown makes salient these states, along with the inherently transient quality of our emotional experiences.

Q: I read about projecting "This is a Thought" and the other Thoughts onto Clouds. Why is this helpful?

A: If you are practicing outside and see Clouds, you may find it meaningful to project one or more of the "doing" thoughts and feelings onto them, as it makes more real their fleeting nature. As the clouds move along, you'll sense that so too do the Thoughts and Feelings.

Q: The Tree exercise primarily involves adjusting the posture. It also seems that stretching the fingers is important too. Does it matter which I do?

A: One reason for the "finger stretching" option is that you may be in a position where it is not easy to adjust the posture (e.g., sitting or reclining). In this case, stretching and relaxing the fingers (which resemble the side branches of the Tree) can be a meaningful engagement of the body. It can also feel good. When walking or standing, adjusting the posture tends to work well and can be sufficient, though both can be helpful and done relatively quickly.

Q: I notice that most of the exercises begin with the Tree. Is there a reason for that?

A: Many mindfulness practices begin with the Body. Because the Tree represents the Body, the SoBe Mindful exercises start there. Doing so can be grounding and stabilizing and set a solid foundation for practice.

Q: Can I practice the SoBe Mindful Minute without the *doing* part? Sometimes I feel like going straight to the "awareness / *being*" part.

A: Yes. In fact, punctuated practices tend to arise spontaneously, and if you are naturally engaging the *being* aspect of practice, it might even be a little jarring to shift to *doing*. In general, the state of mind and body you are experiencing in the moment (e.g., anxious, relaxed, engaged) will naturally guide you into a form of practice that is responsive to the moment.

Q: Why are the Butterfly and Bird Elements only regarded as *being* Elements?

A: Both listening and feeling grateful have qualities that arise spontaneously. Because birds and butterflies will often appear out of nowhere, their very natures lend themselves more readily to "dropping into Awareness," as opposed to making an effort.

Q: Do you recommend that I only practice the exercises in the book, or should I also practice other mindfulness exercises?

A: You are strongly encouraged to look at the larger landscape of mindfulness practices and practice those that you find meaningful. Ideally, the SoBe Mindful Method will enrich your experience with these practices and they, in turn, will deepen your capacity to experience moments of punctuated mindfulness. The SoBe Mindful Sunrise and the SoBe Mindful Minute, as noted below, are designed to seamlessly flow into one or more traditional mindfulness practices.

Q: Is there a way to bridge the SoBe Mindful practices with traditional mindfulness exercises?

A: Yes. First, you can look to the SoBe Mindful book series for book-guided versions of traditional mindfulness practices, like the body scan, breath awareness, and bare attention practices. Second, a planned practice, like the SoBe Mindful Sunrise, can naturally segue into a traditional practice. For example, when the Sun rises and shines on the Tree, you can transition to a body scan; when the Sun shines on the Wind, you can transition to a breath awareness practice; when the Sun shines on Clouds, you can transition to a labeling or awareness of emotions practice; and when attention moves to the Sun, you can practice open monitoring.

Q: Since the Wind/Breath is an Element and also something that is arising all the time, it can be confusing to pay attention to an Element, like the Tree, and be aware of breathing. What should I do when I am aware of the Wind at the same time I am focusing on the Tree?

A: On the one hand, all of the Elements are arising all the time, and your observation is one that suggests you are more fully aware. To the extent you find that this interferes with your practice, see if you can move your sense of the Breath into the background of Awareness. In this way it is present, but not dominant.

Q: Sometimes when I am outside I see so many trees I can get overwhelmed. Any suggestions?

A: If you are feeling overwhelmed by a lot of trees, it may be that you are trying to "do" a practice each time you see a tree. If this happens, try shifting your perspective so that you feel connected to the community of trees, as opposed to separate from them. This may allow the trees to cue a more sustained adjusted posture and body awareness without it feeling overwhelming or like a series of different tasks.

Q: Sometimes when I am practicing the SoBe Mindful Minute I feel rushed—like I am trying to get through all of the Elements in a hurry. This doesn't seem mindful.

A: It can be a common experience to feel rushed, especially if one approaches the exercise as something to "do." This may reveal a feeling of "urgency" not limited to this exercise, but which follows you around during the day—and may contribute to feeling stressed and anxious. Of course, in practicing this exercise, there is no rush or need to hurry. You may find it helpful to spend more time in the *being* mode of practice for each Element.

Q: There are other elements that I can think of that could be included, like the ocean and mountains. Why weren't they included, and is it okay if I use them?

A: The SoBe Mindful Method is based on natural elements that everyone in the world, no matter where they live, experience on a fairly regular basis. The ocean and mountains fall outside this condition, but certainly could be meaningful cues, and you can comfortably expand the horizon of elements. In fact, doing so can be especially profound since it emanates from your own experience and insight. Pay attention, though, to your motivation, and keep it simple. Sometimes we make things more complex as a way to escape the present moment; more doing. So, keep it simple.

Recommended Reading

Books

André, Christophe, *Looking at Mindfulness: 25 Ways to Live in the Moment Through Art* (Blue Rider Press, 2015).

Coleman, Mark, *Awake in the Wild: Mindfulness in Nature as a Path of Self-Discovery* (New World Library, 2006).

Harris, Dan, *10% Happier: How I Tamed the Voice in My Head, Reduced Stress Without Losing My Edge, and Found Self-Help That Actually Works—A True Story* (Dey Street Books, 2014).

Harris, Sam, *Waking Up: A Guide to Spirituality Without Religion* (Simon & Schuster, 2014).

Kabat-Zinn, Jon, *Mindfulness for Beginners: Reclaiming the Present Moment—and Your Life* (Sounds True, 2016).

Nhat Hanh, Thich, *Present Moment Wonderful Moment: Mindfulness Verses for Daily Living* (Parallax Press, 2002).

Ryan, Tim, *A Mindful Nation: How a Simple Practice Can Help Us Reduce Stress, Improve Performance, and Recapture the American Spirit* (Hay House, 2012).

Salzberg, Sharon, *Real Happiness: The Power of Meditation: A 28-Day Program* (Workman Publishing Company, 2010).

Shapiro, Shauna & Linda Carlson, *The Art and Science of Mindfulness: Integrating Mindfulness Into Psychology and the Helping Professions* (APA, 2017).

Tolle, Eckhart, *Stillness Speaks* (New World Library, 2003).

Williams, Mark, John Teasdale, Zindel Segal, & Jon Kabat-Zinn, *The Mindful Way Through Depression: Freeing Yourself from Chronic Unhappiness* (The Guilford Press, 2012).

Magazine

Mindful (mindful.org).

About the Author

Scott Rogers, MS, JD, is founder and director of the Institute for Mindfulness Studies, which he founded in 2003 to share mindfulness in accessible, enjoyable, and meaningful forms. A nationally recognized leader in the field, Scott founded and directs the country's first Mindfulness in Law program at the University of Miami School of Law and co-founded the University of Miami's Mindfulness Research and Practice Initiative, where he collaborates on neuroscience research, exploring the enduring brain and behavior changes that may accompany mindfulness-training programs. Scott is principal advisor to Innergy Meditation Studio in Miami Beach.

Since 1999, Scott has taught mindfulness to more than ten thousand people, including athletes, accountants, bankers, business leaders, children, educators, financial advisors, firefighters, judges, lawyers, law students, mediators, medical students, nurses, parents, physicians, and therapists. His books are among the first integrating mindfulness across disciplines; his website, themindfulparent.org, was the first to explore the relationship between mindfulness and parenting, and themindfullawyer.com was the first to explore mindfulness and law. He is creator of *Jurisight,* the first program in the country to integrate mindfulness, law, and neuroscience research. Scott created the mindfulness programs Worrier to Warrior, Wanting to Wisdom, and SoBe Mindful. He conducts presentations and workshops across the country and is known for his energetic engagement sharing mindfulness with audiences.

Scott is author of five books, including *Mindful Parenting: Meditations, Verses & Visualization for a More Joyful Life, Mindfulness for Law Students: Using the Power of Mindful Awareness to Achieve Balance and Success in Law School, The Six-Minute Solution: A Mindfulness Primer for Attorneys, Mindfulness and*

Professional Responsibility: A Guidebook for Integrating Mindfulness into the Law School Curriculum, and the CDs *Attending: A Physician's Introduction to Mindfulness*, and *Mindfulness, Balance & The Lawyer's Brain*.

Scott lectures across the country, speaks at law, medical, leadership, and scientific conferences, and has appeared on television, *HuffPost*, and National Public Radio, and been interviewed in the *Wall Street Journal*, the *Miami Herald*, the *National Law Journal, Mindful Magazine, Shambhala Sun*, and other newspapers and magazines for his work on mindfulness.

Scott lives in Miami Beach, Florida, with his wife, Pam, and two daughters, Millie and Rose.

About the Illustrator

Cathy Gibbs Thornton is a graphic designer and illustrator with over thirty years of experience in the creative, advertising, and printing industries. Originally from Barbados, Cathy studied art and advertising in Miami, graduating summa cum laude with both her associate's and bachelor of arts degrees in advertising communications. She worked as a senior designer, art director, and creative director for large advertising agencies in Barbados and in Miami before opening her own business, CG Graphics.

Over the years, Cathy's award-winning artwork has been featured in several publications, including the *Miami Herald* and the cover of *South Florida* magazine. Cathy takes pride in working closely with her clients from a wide range of industries in the United States, Canada, and throughout the Caribbean region, helping them achieve their creative goals. Her illustrations encompass both traditional and digital media, and her design capabilities include two- and three-dimensional designs. She specializes in logo, brochure, and ad design. Local examples of her work in the Miami area include the official logos for the Village of Palmetto Bay and the Town of Cutler Bay, both award-winning competition entries.

Cathy and her husband Mike, a multimedia specialist and writer, live in Orlando, Florida. Their daughter Natasha is a cinematographer/editor working with the University of South Florida, and their late son Jason was a graduate student at the University of Central Florida, studying psychology and neuroscience.

SoBe Mindful® Tools and Toys

The SoBe Mindful Method becomes increasingly useful and effective the more the Elements are practiced and reinforced. For this reason, there are a variety of SoBe Mindful reminders that you can use to help support your practice. These include:

SoBe Mindful Magnets—Each contains an image of one or more of the Elements. Place these on your refrigerator or other locations so that they may reinforce your connection to the Elements and also provide frequent wake-up reminders.

SoBe Mindful Coloring Books—You can color in the Elements, both to soothe away stress and to engage the SoBe Mindful Method. Coloring becomes the mindfulness practice, as images of the Elements cue waking up. You can find coloring books with imagery found in this book, as well as with images of Elements local to your part of the world.

SoBe Mindful Stickers—Place these colorful stickers in strategic places where you will come across them during the day to serve as wake-up reminders.

SoBe Mindful Guided Practice Recordings—Recorded practices that introduce you to the Elements and guide you through mindfulness-oriented sensualizations and visualizations.

SoBe Mindful Blocks—Each panel of these six-sided blocks contains an image of one of the Elements. Adults and teenagers can place the cube on their work or study desk, or a table, to be reminded to practice during the day. Ideal for playing creative and fun mindfulness games with young children. Comes in different sizes and materials.

SoBe Mindful Website—Offers instruction, blog postings, video and audio guided practices, workshops, and general information about the SoBe Mindful Method. www.SoBeMindful.com

SoBe Mindful Social Media—Online resources to connect with members of the SoBe Mindful community, and keep up with SoBe Mindful resources, tips, and practices.

Instagram: SoBeMindful
Twitter: @SoBeMindful
Facebook: SoBeMindful

Coming Soon

SoBe Mindful App—Offers a wide variety of SoBe Mindful practice options, including self-guided practices, guided recordings, and daily cues with the Elements.

SoBe Mindful Practice Cards—A set of colorful cards that depicts the Elements by themselves and in combination to learn and reinforce the SoBe Mindful Method.

SoBe Mindful Book Series—Provides readers of all ages with a selection of practices that integrate mindfulness into various aspects of everyday life. Book titles include:

SoBe Mindful with Children
SoBe Mindful while Sitting
SoBe Mindful on Vacation
SoBe Mindful at Home
SoBe Mindful and Aging
SoBe Mindful while Sad
SoBe Mindful in Nature
SoBe Mindful when Sick
SoBe Mindful at School

www.ingramcontent.com/pod-product-compliance
Lightning Source LLC
Chambersburg PA
CBHW040324300426
44112CB00021B/2869